]

of

LOVE

The BOOKS of HEAVEN on EARTH

Volume One

Written by Daniel Prok

More Books from Daniel Prok

Connect to God's Love, Light and Heaven

within Yourself through All of

"The BOOKS of HEAVEN on EARTH":

"The BOOK of LOVE"

"The BOOK of LIGHT"

"The BOOK of HEAVEN"

"The BOOK of LIFE"

"El LIBRO del AMOR"

Get them now as Paperback or Ebooks online
and from bookstores everywhere.

Get the audiobooks on Audible, iTunes and more.

For bulk purchase orders and to have Daniel speak to
your organization contact him through social media or
www.DanielProk.com.

The

BOOK

of

LOVE

The BOOK of LOVE

For permissions requests, speaking inquiries, and bulk purchase options contact Daniel Prok at...

www.DanielProk.com

ISBN-13: 9798567844847

Printed in the United States of America

TABLE OF CONTENTS

The BOOK of LOVE

Introduction

A message from Jesus through Daniel

It is a great honor and privilege to share this message of Love with you.

I didn't realize that I was on a life journey of Love until a few weeks before I received this Divine writing from Jesus the Christ directly into my mind for me to share with you.

The journey of Love I have been on for the last 10 years has taken me from not loving myself, to self-love, to loving myself completely, to feeling loving and loveable to others, to feeling loved and adored by God, and most recently practicing being someone who loves all the time.

All these layers and definitions of Love that I have been practicing and experiencing have improved my life tremendously... and then I received this Divine message of Love from Jesus!

"But how do we know that it's Jesus?", you may ask.

I know from the way the message came into my mind, and then through my heart and soul. The warmth of the Loving energy of Jesus is beyond anything I have felt in my human form. Also, these words are so Divinely stated that it is beyond me to come up with something this good!

As for you, you will have a knowing as you read the words. Feel them with your Heart and Soul. Feel them with the depths of your being. You will know.

This message takes God's Love, and God's Love within you, to a greater level of understanding, knowing, depth and expansion.

Thank you to Jesus for sharing this beautiful message so that everyone, everywhere can experience the Love of God in the way that he has.

God Bless you all with God's Love!

Daniel Prok

Chapter One

A message of Love from Jesus

My Beloved,

It is with great Love that I share these ideas with you.

To understand Love is to BE Love. It is not fathomable by the human mind to know the depths of the Love that can be expressed by the Creator of All that is. In the Heavenly Realms, Unconditional Love is the way society works. On Earth it is something less than that.

But know that the practice and habituation of being loving, being caring, being compassionate, having peace in your mind, connecting to your Soul, connecting to your Divinity; all these things contribute to carrying the vibration of Love in all aspects of who you are as a human, and all aspects of your Divinity, your Christ Consciousness, your purity, your oneness with everything.

As I have demonstrated to you and for all of humanity; to express, feel and BE Love under the most stressful of situations that one could imagine for a human life.

Feeling God's Divine Love, radiating that Divine Love, showing that Divine Love, expressing that Divine Love... even while being rebuked publicly for something that wasn't true, even while being condemned publicly in front of the masses, even while being punished, tormented, spit upon, yelled at, cursed at, and even while having a crown of thorns placed on my head, and being nailed to the cross at Calvary.

Even during those times, the Love of the Creator was in all aspects of my being.

What looked horrific from an external perspective, and from your perspective, to me was just an experience that was overridden by a knowing within me.

A knowing of God's Love,

Eternal Love,

Unconditional Love.

The most radiant, purest vibrational frequency of Love that was so strongly in my knowing that even the perception of death on a cross could not stop the eternal constant Love of God shining from the Core of my Being.

As God is at the Core and Essence

of All of our Beings.

Feeling that eternal, everlasting, infinite and always expanding Love of God in those moments.

And, as I rose again from perceived death, as death is only a construct that the human mind has created, the feeling of Love radiates and saturates my Eternal Being, as it radiates and saturates your Eternal Being.

You are never separated from that Love.

You are always completely one with that Love.

Anything that you may experience that is different than that most beautiful, glorious and wonderful Loving energy that IS our Heavenly Father, and our Divine Mother and the Creator of All that is... is an illusion... is a misperception. Your connection to that Love is Divine, is constant, and is permanent from your Soul's perspective.

But as life has happened in your human form, you have learned through experience not to believe in that Love. More importantly you have been strategically conditioned by certain forces and powers in this world, to believe more in what you see with your eyes and hear with your ears than to believe in the truth.

To believe beyond the illusion of the

experience of your life in your unique reality...

To believe in something that you can't see

or hear or touch or taste or smell...

But to believe in something

that you can Feel!

You can feel it in your Heart.

You can know it in your Soul.

And that loving embrace of the Creator
that is always there for you
has been conditioned out of you
during your human experience.

But this book is written to take you on your path and guide you. It is a path with many twists and turns and undulations. The road is paved at times; the road is rough at times. But the road that you are traveling is a road within yourself. A road that goes to the Core of your Being. A road that is eternally more beautiful and glorious as you continue on your Divine path, connecting more and more to your own Divinity.

The BOOK of LOVE

God within You.

Your Christ Consciousness.

Your Beauty. Your Fulfillment.

Your Strength. Your Courage.

Your Peace. Your Love.

Your Joy.

All these things are within You!

They are expressed into the world around you in many different ways, but all the greatest qualities and characteristic of the Creator... God, Yahweh, Jehovah Jireh, the Christ, Christ Consciousness; all these personalities of God, all these characteristics of God, are right there within your Divine Consciousness.

Your Eternalness.

Your Divinity.

Coming from a place of knowing
the Love inside of you.

That stillness within you can be the peace that passes all understanding, and is the truest nature of yourself. Your true nature is to Love. Your true nature is wellness and well-being. Your true Divine nature is radiant Joy... is exuberant Bliss... that is your true nature!

And the more that you connect with your Soul, your Heart, your Higher Self, your Godself, your Christ Consciousness, and the Christ within me... the more that you connect with all of these... the more you will be able to create the life, and a World, that is as the original Creator's plan for this Earth Paradise.

This Heavenly Realm is right there,
right where you are at!

Right in the middle of your Consciousness!

And when that vibration is the frequency that you hold as your natural state, and habitual and chronic state within your human experience; when you maintain that energetic frequency coding, your Divine Coding, your Divine Blueprint, there is only the purity of this vibration deep within you.

And as you send that energy from the Core of your Being through all aspects of yourself, the reality that you experience, as well as the reality for the collective experience on Earth, transforms.

God has always wanted
Glorious things for his Children.

God Shines an Adoring Gaze
upon You at All times!

God has never left you, will never leave you, will never forsake you. God is always there with you, but it can be easy for the mind to believe in a disconnection because we are so accustomed to trusting in our physical senses... when Love is beyond that.

It is with Great Joy that I share this Book of Love with you!

I am eternally here at your service to guide you on your journey back to Oneness with the Almighty.

Jesus the Christ

Divine Decrees of Love

I AM Always with You.

I AM Eternal and Everlasting Love for You.

I AM Love Beyond Measure.

I AM God in Action.

I AM that I AM.

I AM Everlasting Peace in your Heart and Mind.

I AM Upliftment in the times of Sorrow.

The BOOK of LOVE

I AM Radiant Joy in the midst of Perceived Chaos.

I AM Supernatural Exultation of the
Heavenly Host of Angels and Archangels.

I AM the Joy of God.

I AM Infinite Peace in a Moment of Disbelief.

I AM Eternal Blessings and Favor Beyond Measure.

I AM Radiant Love that Saturates my Entire Being.

The BOOK of LOVE

I AM Wondrous Gifts given as my
Divine Birthright.

I AM the Sacred Heart Flame of Jesus Christ.

I AM Blessed with Hosannas in the Highest.

I AM Eternal and Unconditional
Love and Gratitude.

I AM the Prince of Peace.

I AM Glory to God in the Highest.

The BOOK of LOVE

As the Angels and Archangels join us in exultation,
we laud and, magnify, and amplify...

the Christ within You...

the Love within You...

the Peace within You...

the Joy within You...

the Happiness...

the Fun...

the Laughter...

the Good Times...

the Special Moments...

All of those things that you experience, are
experiences that the Creator is having with you!

Loving with you,

laughing with you,

sharing with you,

serving with you,

caring with you,

uplifting with you,

enjoying with you...

and again,

Loving with you!

And Loving You so much, and adoring You so much,
and caring for You so much... that it is my duty to
guide you into that "KNOWING" for yourself and for
all of humanity.

The BOOK of LOVE

I AM Infinite Blessings and Great Joy...
and I AM Eternally yours!

My Love for you is Everlasting and Unconditional.

My Love for you Never Ends.

My Love for you Always has been
and Always Will Be.

I AM Love, as YOU also are Love.

God Bless Us All Now and Forever!

Amen and Amen!

Chapter Two

Love is something that you ARE

As with many things in life, Love seems to be elusive.

Love seems to be something that comes and goes, like the waves crashing on the beach. The waves come in and crash, and the waves go back out, only to come back again.

An ebb and flow that occurs naturally in the ocean, but the ebb and flow of Love that occurs in a human's life... the perception of not having Love, the perception of experiencing Love for moments at a time, the perspective of being in Love and having that wondrous feeling continue for an extended period of time... only to have it fade away like that wave in the ocean as it drifts back into the sea.

The experience of Love like that in your life is only due to living a life where you trust more in your physical senses than you trust in your Divinity.

When you trust in, believe in, and know your Divinity... you trust in, believe in, and know that God's Love is there in your Heart, in your Soul, in your Body, in your Mind, in your Emotions, in your Godself, in your Higher Self.

That Love is always in all aspects of you, but to live in that "knowing" can be perceived by many as a challenge.

What we see and hear looks so real and sounds so real. Looks to be the truth and sounds like knowledge. But in the ever changing reality and life that you live, what looks and sounds like something that is other than Love is just a perception of life. It is not Divine truth.

Reality and life in the way that you experience it seems to be very meaningful. But it is important for you to understand that you are giving meaning to life's experiences from the point of view of your programmed mental body. You perceive the world in certain ways because you were raised in certain environments which created those perceptions.

To perceive things the way that God perceives them is a beautiful thing. To perceive things and resonate with unconditional Love is a learned behavior for someone who has been conditioned to not live in that vibration.

But you are not learning something
that you don't already know!

It is one thing to learn about, and be educated in a field of endeavor that you haven't had experience in from the point of view of your life... your human life that you are living.

But when we talk about Love... Love is not something that you need to learn, it is something that you ARE.

It may seem like you need to learn to be Loving, learn to be at Peace, learn to be filled with God's Joy. It may seem like you need to learn those things but that is a misperception of absolute truth, because you already ARE those things.

You are God's Love.

You are Peace Beyond Measure.

And you are Joyous Exultation!

That is your Natural State.

That is the natural state of your true self, of your Godself, of your Soul, and of your Heart. And to realize that living in a life where one experiences things other than Love should really be looked at as poor role modeling, bad modeling of behaviors, untrue perceptions of reality... where one grows up learning anger, learning to be afraid, learning to be ashamed of themselves and their bodies, learning that they are not good enough, learning that they are imperfect, learning that they are sinners.

God only makes Perfect Things!

God's level of planning, and meticulously-detailed blueprints for the Divine construction of your Consciousness, the Divine construction of your human body, the Divine construction of the world you live in... it has been pristinely created with magnificence.

Where things have gone awry is with the way that the human mind has been coerced into believing in imperfections, believing in lies, believing in lack, believing in disempowering emotions, believing that the world is a dangerous place, when all of that is simply a negatively skewed perception.

When you align with your Divinity, you align with your Divine Blueprint, you align with your Christ Consciousness, you begin to believe in the perfection that is YOU and the perfection that is the world around you.

There is only Love.

And within Love are variations
that are also enjoyable to experience...

Peace,

Joy,

Freedom,

Laughter,

Exuberance,

Bliss,

Ecstasy...

a truly Elated and Glorious state of being.

All those things are Love.

To Love...

...with Love as your most beautiful state of being; to live in Love, to Love, to be Loved, to have Love, to feel Love, to know Love, to express Love, to think Lovingly... all those things are the truths of your existence.

To Love for no other reason but to Love.

To Love because you are Love.

To Love because your Soul Loves.

To Love as your Heart Loves.

28

The BOOK of LOVE

To Love yourself and others
as God Loves yourself and others.

Love at all times...

Love in all experiences...

Saturating everything,
everywhere throughout
all space and time,
and all of Creation...

All of it is Love.

To know that,

to remember that,

to feel that,

to be that,

is a beautiful and

wonderful thing.

And it is always there for you
as I AM always there for you.

Love never fails.

Love always is Victorious.

Love is Constant and Everlasting.

The flow of Love in your life is Eternal.

Divine Decrees of Love

I AM the Love of the World.

I AM the Love of a Million Billion Mother Earths.

I AM Love Everlasting and Ever Blasting.

I AM Love to the Core of my Being.

I AM Love in Every Eternal Moment.

I AM Love Amplified Times Infinity.

The BOOK of LOVE

I AM Love Radiating for all Eternity.

I AM Love in the Hearts and Minds
of All Sentient Beings.

I AM Love at the Core of Mother Earth.

I AM Love in the Eternalness of Infinity.

I AM Love as seen in a Mother's gaze
upon her New Born Child.

I AM Love Expressed Openly and Confidently.

I AM Love to be Experienced in Infinite Ways.

The BOOK of LOVE

I AM Love to be Increased and Expanded Eternally.

I AM Love in my Body, Mind and Spirit.

I AM Love from the Heart of Jesus Christ.

I AM Love in the Highest Vibrations
of all of Creation.

I AM Love that Seeks no Retribution.

I AM Love in All my Interactions.

I AM Love Eternally and Evermore.

The BOOK of LOVE

I AM Love Amplified by the Hearts of the
Archangels and the Heavenly Host.

I AM Love that needs no Loving response.

I AM Love that Gives to those who need it.

I AM Love. I AM Love. I AM Pure Love.

I AM God's Wondrous Love for all of Humanity.

I AM Love in its Purest Form.

I AM that I AM.

Chapter Three

God's Love is Beyond Measure

God's Love is Beyond Measure. But the Love that you experience in this lifetime is more like a glass of water. When you are thirsty, you drink from the glass and it quenches your thirst, but soon enough life happens and you are thirsty again. Looking to fill up that glass of water once more.

While all the while there is an ocean that is deep and vast, and has all the water one could ever want or need or desire. But living life in your current vibrational frequency condition, you are unaware of the ocean with the everlasting supply.

You have access to this Ocean of Love.

The Love that you can experience has no ending in the ways that it can manifest in your reality.

But to continue your life, seeking a reason to Love, looking for someone to Love, needing an experience that feels like Love... all these things are a part of the experience of conditional Love that you have grown accustomed to.

But the more that you become aware of, and tap into, the permanent loving vibration at the Core of your Being... the Love within your Heart, the Love within your Soul, the Love within your Christ Consciousness... you move from living in that cycle where you thirst and then seek, need and desire to have that thirst quenched.

When the ocean of God's Love is right there in your Heart all along, is right there in your Divinity, is right there in the Core of your Being.

You have never been separate from it, and it is so vast that you cannot even fathom the immensity of the Love that God has for you and has for all of Creation.

Love beyond measure,

means Love that could not be measured

by any means of calculation.

You cannot quantify God's Love, and you cannot quantify the Love that you have inside of yourself as your natural state of being; your true natural self.

The Love of the Christ within your Heart is always there as a permanent construct, but the mind has learned so many patterns that restrict the flow of God's Love in your life. The mind can pinch off that flow that is like a river that is flowing powerfully, and twists, and turns, and moves over all obstructions. The mind can be like a dam and put up permanent obstructions to that energy, so that the Love that is always available, always flowing, and always inside of you... that Love is only trickling through your consciousness.

When it could be a mighty roaring river of Love flowing through your Heart, through your Mind, through your Body, through your Emotions, through your Soul and Spirit. The mighty river of Love that is always there, but you are the one who has learned to pinch it off with your thinking... with your mind.

The BOOK of LOVE

When you live in your Divinity, when you live in your Heart and your Christ Consciousness, there is that ocean, that deep, immense Ocean of God's Love.

Bask in it, bathe in it, saturate your entire being with it.

Feel that in all aspects of your Being.

Feel Gods' Love.

God's Radiant Glorious Love.

Feel it in your Smile.

Feel it as you Gaze into your own Eyes in a mirror.

The BOOK of LOVE

Feel it in your Body.

Feel it in your Heart and Soul.

And condition your mind to
Feel, Be, and Know God's Love.

Love Beyond Measure.

God's Love is Beyond Measure.

Divine Decrees of Love

I AM Love Beyond Measure.

I AM Love in the Highest of Vibrations.

I AM Love at the Core of my Being.

I AM Love in the Crystalline Core of Mother Earth.

I AM Love in the Crystal Core of My Godself.

I AM the Love of a Mother and her Child.

I AM the Love of a Father and his Son.

The BOOK of LOVE

I AM the Love of the Sacred Heart of Christ.

I AM the Love of God's Heart
Beating with Eternal Perfection.

I AM Love with the Glory of the Angels.

I AM Love that Passes all Understanding.

I AM Love that fills the Hearts and Minds
of Everyone on Earth.

I AM the Love of a Billion Trillion Mother Earths.

I AM the Eternal Love of the
Heavenly Host of Angels and Archangels.

The BOOK of LOVE

I AM Love in its most Beautiful Manifestation.

I AM the Love of a Mother's Gaze
at her New Born Child.

I AM the Love of God's Greatest Creation.

I AM Love Beyond Measure.

I AM Love with Increasing
Frequency and Vibration.

I AM Love Everlasting and Ever Blasting.

I AM Love Pulsing in the Heartbeat of God.

The BOOK of LOVE

I AM the Love of the Christ within Me.

I AM Love in its Eternal Perfection.

I AM Pure Love that Saturates
the Entirety of God's Creation.

I AM Love Beyond Measure.

I AM Love as God's Hidden Treasure within Me.

I AM Love Expressed in Infinite Ways.

I AM Love in All of My Perceptions.

I AM Love.

I AM Love Beyond Measure.

Final Words

To experience God's Love as your permanent state of being is a beautiful thing!

And that permanent state of being with its most wonderful, perfect and uplifting vibration, is permanently increasing in frequency, amplitude and vibration.

God's Love keeps expanding.

The depths of God's Love are Eternal.

The upliftment of God's Love never ends.

The Christ within You, and the Love of the Christ within You, is always there for You.

My Love is always there for You.

I AM Always there to help You to feel the Love that is already within You.

The BOOK of LOVE

While God's Love is in everything,
for your experience of Love,
all you have to do is go within.

Live in your Heart.

Live in your Soul.

Live in your Divine Blueprint.

Live in your Christ Consciousness.

Live in God's Love which is Love Beyond Measure.

Live in the Ocean of God's Love
and experience the immensity of that.

Experience it in this present moment.

And I bless you with the anchoring of that vibration, that loving energy, that elated, blissful feeling.

I bless you, as we reset your system to align with your Divinity, and your Oneness with the Love of God that is YOU, and always has been YOU, and always will be YOU.

You are God's Love.

You are God's Light.

You are God's Infinite Perfection.

You are God's Eternal Well-being.

Divine Decrees of Love

I AM the Ocean of God's Love.

I AM the Love of Jesus Christ.

I AM the Sacred Heart Fire Love of Elohim.

I AM Love Divine.

I AM Love Sublime.

I AM Love Everlasting and Ever Blasting.

I AM Love in its Purest Perfection.

I AM Love and the Immensity of its Expression.

I AM Love Eternal and Everlasting.

I AM Love in God's Highest State of Consciousness.

I AM Love.

I AM Love.

I AM Love.

Closing message from Jesus the Christ

From my Heart to your Heart, I send this message of Love so that you experience God's Love the way that I have experienced God's Love.

I give you God's Love in its highest form.

And it is always there within You, and I AM always with You.

I Love You Eternally.

I Love You with Great Joy!

And I Bless You with God's Love Beyond Measure.

Jesus of Nazareth

The Christ

About the Author

Daniel Prok is a God and Jesus loving
actor, life coach, model, speaker, writer and leader
who is creating Heaven on Earth.

He resides in La Jolla, California
and Sedona, Arizona.

For more content from Daniel to
improve your life go to...

www.DanielProk.com

Also, subscribe to Daniel Prok on Youtube.

And, follow Daniel Prok on Social Media.

More Books from Daniel Prok

Connect to God's Love, Light and Heaven

within Yourself through All of

"The BOOKS of HEAVEN on EARTH":

"The BOOK of LOVE"

"The BOOK of LIGHT"

"The BOOK of HEAVEN"

"The BOOK of LIFE"

"El LIBRO del AMOR"

Get them now as Paperback or Ebooks online
and from bookstores everywhere.

Get the audiobooks on Audible, iTunes and more.

For bulk purchase orders and to have Daniel speak to
your organization contact him through social media or
www.DanielProk.com.

Thank You!

Thank You!

Thank You...

In advance for sharing a positive review of this book with all the people that you love, on Amazon.com, as well as on your favorite social media platforms like Facebook, Instagram and others.

Your voice matters in helping us promote a positive message that will fill the hearts, minds and lives of all of God's People with...

Love, Light and Heaven...

And create Heaven on Earth for the Collective.

Share the Message

The words in this book are so powerful that as you read, embody and live this message you will create a literal Heaven on Earth for yourself and for your LIFE.

And now is the time to Go Forth, as Jesus has said, and Share this message with the world as we create Heaven on Earth for the Collective.

Share these concepts with friends and loved ones.

Give books to your family and friends.

Give books as gifts for Christmas.

Supply books for your church,
schools and organizations.

Be the Light that lights the path in the lives of those around you, as we experience this beautiful Planet Earth, the Garden of Eden, as is the Original Plan for our glorious home.

I Love you and I Bless you!

Daniel Prok

Printed in Great Britain
by Amazon

17391811R00037